For My Father

GIANT SEA CREATURES

by Edith Kunhardt / illustrated by Fiona Reid

Prentice K. Stout, Consultant
Marine Education Specialist, University of Rhode Island

A GOLDEN BOOK · NEW YORK
Western Publishing Company, Inc., Racine, Wisconsin 53404

Contents

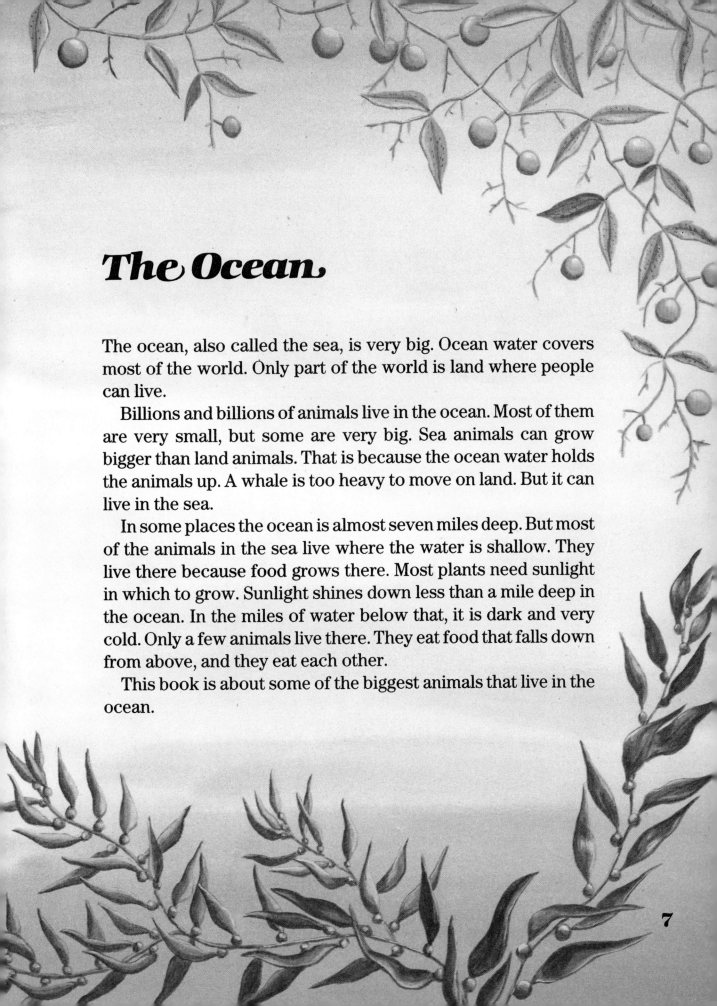

The Ocean

The ocean, also called the sea, is very big. Ocean water covers most of the world. Only part of the world is land where people can live.

Billions and billions of animals live in the ocean. Most of them are very small, but some are very big. Sea animals can grow bigger than land animals. That is because the ocean water holds the animals up. A whale is too heavy to move on land. But it can live in the sea.

In some places the ocean is almost seven miles deep. But most of the animals in the sea live where the water is shallow. They live there because food grows there. Most plants need sunlight in which to grow. Sunlight shines down less than a mile deep in the ocean. In the miles of water below that, it is dark and very cold. Only a few animals live there. They eat food that falls down from above, and they eat each other.

This book is about some of the biggest animals that live in the ocean.

MERMAID AND MERMAN

Long ago, people believed in mermaids and mermen. A mermaid was supposed to be half-woman, half-fish. A merman was half-man, half-fish. Did sailors who saw the sea cow, or dugong, get mixed up?

DUGONG

NESSIE

Nessie is a sea monster that is supposed to live in Scotland's deep lake called Loch Ness. People in boats, planes, and submarines have searched for the Loch Ness monster, but no one has ever found it.

Sea Monsters

People have always made up stories about strange sea creatures. Sometimes the sea monsters in the stories look something like real sea animals.

Sailors thought they saw sea serpents in the water with their coils moving up and down. Could they have seen some dolphins following each other? Or some seaweed floating on the water? Or a sea snake? Or a whale?

SEA SNAKE

SEA SERPENT

SEAWEED

KRAKEN

Another kind of sea monster was called the kraken. It was like a huge octopus or squid. There were stories that the kraken attacked large sailing ships and ripped them apart, throwing everyone into the sea.

OCTOPUS

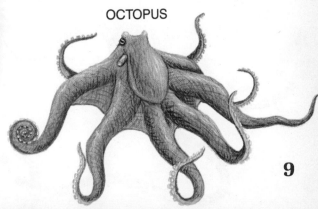

9

Creatures of the Very Shallow Seas

RIBBON WORM   The ribbon worm can grow to be 90 feet long. In the daytime, it lives in the mud of the sea bottom. At night, it hunts for food. The ribbon worm eats other sea worms, shrimp, snails, and small fish. It captures its food with a sticky tube that has a pointed end. Some ribbon worms have a poison dagger on the end of the tube.

The body of the ribbon worm can break apart by itself. Each part becomes a new worm.

There are many kinds of ribbon worms. Some of them are only two feet long. Some of them are brightly colored. They can be yellow, orange, red, brown, or green. They can have stripes or a pattern. Ribbon worms are very thin–like a long, thin string. The longest ones are as long as 540 earthworms end to end.

Ribbon worms can live a year without food if they cannot find food.

It would take 540 earthworms to make up the length of one ribbon worm.

GIANT CLAM The giant clam has a soft body inside two shells. It can be four feet wide and can weigh 500 pounds. It lives on the ocean bottom in warm water.

The giant clam is so heavy that it cannot move. Small hairs on its body fan food into its mouth. It feeds on tiny sea plants. If an enemy comes along, the clam shuts its shells tightly.

MORAY EEL The moray eel can be ten feet long. It looks like a snake, but it is not a snake. It is a fish. It has no scales on its body. It lives in rocky holes in the day. At night the moray eel swims about and hunts. It catches other fish, crabs, snails, and worms with its sharp teeth.

Moray eels live in rocky holes.

Giant clams are too heavy to move.

11

Creatures of the Shallow Seas

GIANT ARCTIC JELLYFISH   The giant arctic jellyfish may be the longest animal in the sea. Its arms can grow to be 200 feet long.

The giant arctic jellyfish has a body like an open umbrella. It swims by opening and closing the umbrella. Its mouth hangs down from the middle of the umbrella. As many as 800 arms also hang down. The arms are called tentacles and have stingers on them. When a fish swims into the stingers, it cannot move. The tentacles pull the fish up to the mouth of the jellyfish. Then the jellyfish eats the fish.

Jellyfish that sting are dangerous to people. Swimmers have died from touching them. Even the tentacles of dead jellyfish on the beach can be dangerous because the stingers still work. Some jellyfish do not have stingers.

Small jellyfish are not poisonous. People sometimes eat them. Chinese people eat the umbrella and the tentacles. Japanese people wash the umbrella, cut it into pieces, and season it. It tastes like a salted pickle.

TENTACLES

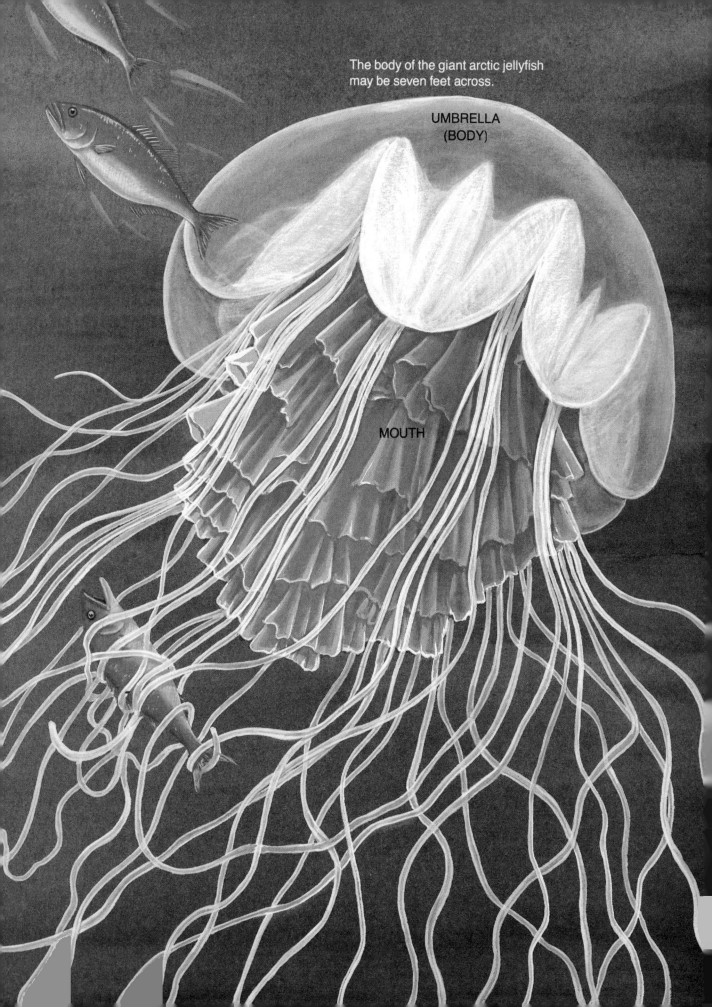

The body of the giant arctic jellyfish may be seven feet across.

UMBRELLA
(BODY)

MOUTH

LEATHERBACK SEA TURTLE The leatherback turtle is bigger than any other turtle on land or in the sea. It can be eight feet long and can weigh 1300 pounds. Its shell is made of small bones covered with a thick, rubbery skin.

Leatherback turtles cannot pull their heads and feet into their shells to escape from enemies. Instead, they swim very fast to get away from their enemies.

Every two or three years female leatherback turtles swim thousands of miles to certain beaches. They go on land at night to lay their eggs. The turtle digs a pit in the sand with her back flippers. She lays about a hundred eggs in the pit. She covers up the hole with sand. Then she goes back to the sea. She never sees her babies.

There are fewer and fewer sea turtles in the ocean each year. Turtles are hunted for their meat and eggs. The leatherback turtle is hunted for an oil made from its skin. Pollution of the ocean is also killing sea turtles.

Many leatherback turtle eggs never hatch because raccoons and people take the eggs from the nests to eat them. Some baby turtles are eaten by sea birds as they crawl to the water. Sometimes crabs and fish eat them after they get to the sea. But there are so many babies that some always escape.

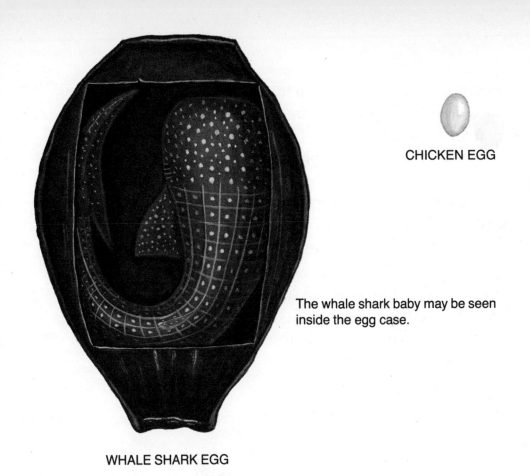

CHICKEN EGG

The whale shark baby may be seen inside the egg case.

WHALE SHARK EGG

WHALE SHARK The whale shark is the biggest shark of all. It is the biggest fish in the world. It can grow to be 60 feet long and can weigh as much as 15 tons.

The whale shark's mouth is not on its underside, like the mouths of other sharks. Its mouth is on the front of its head. It can swim and catch food at the same time. Its mouth is so big two grown-up people can fit in it, but the whale shark does not eat people. It eats tiny animals and plants and small fish. It has many little teeth. It crushes food that is too big to swallow.

Whale sharks swim slowly near the surface of the water, eating food that floats by. They sometimes sleep near the surface of the water. Boats going along at night may run into them.

The whale shark's egg is the biggest egg in the world. It can be as big as 27 inches long and 16 inches around.

A WHALE SHARK'S MOUTH

A SAND SHARK'S
MOUTH

17

GREAT WHITE SHARK The great white shark can grow to be 25 feet long and can weigh 2500 pounds. It sometimes attacks people and sometimes bites small boats. Most of the time it eats sea lions, big fish like tuna, and other sharks. Its large teeth cut as cleanly as a razor.

The great white shark is not really white. It is a lighter gray than other sharks.

This shark cannot breathe if it stops swimming. So it swims all its life without stopping. It can live thirty years.

The great white shark can smell blood in the water from far away. It also has excellent hearing. And it can feel the movements that a dying fish makes in the water. It circles the fish slowly. Then it attacks.

The skin of the great white shark is made of pointed scales and feels like sharp sandpaper. If a swimmer rubbed against a great white shark in the ocean, the person's skin would be torn by the shark's skin.

The great white shark has a skeleton made of cartilage, not bone. The end of a person's nose is made of cartilage.

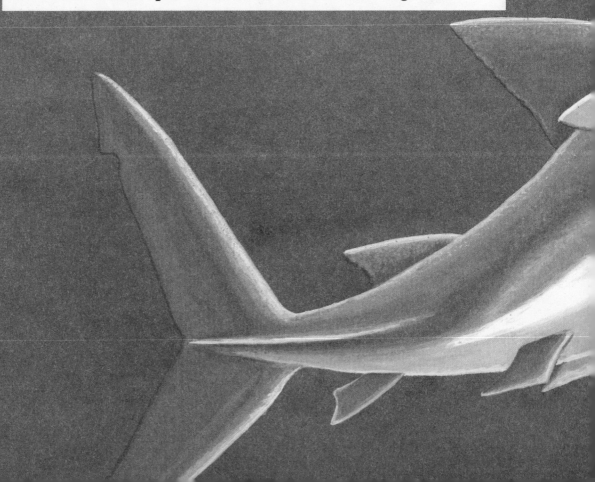

The eye of the great white shark has a covering which can come up to protect it.

The great white shark has two or three rows of teeth. Some other sharks have as many as seven rows. If teeth in the front row break off, new teeth move up. Most sharks grow thousands of teeth in their life.

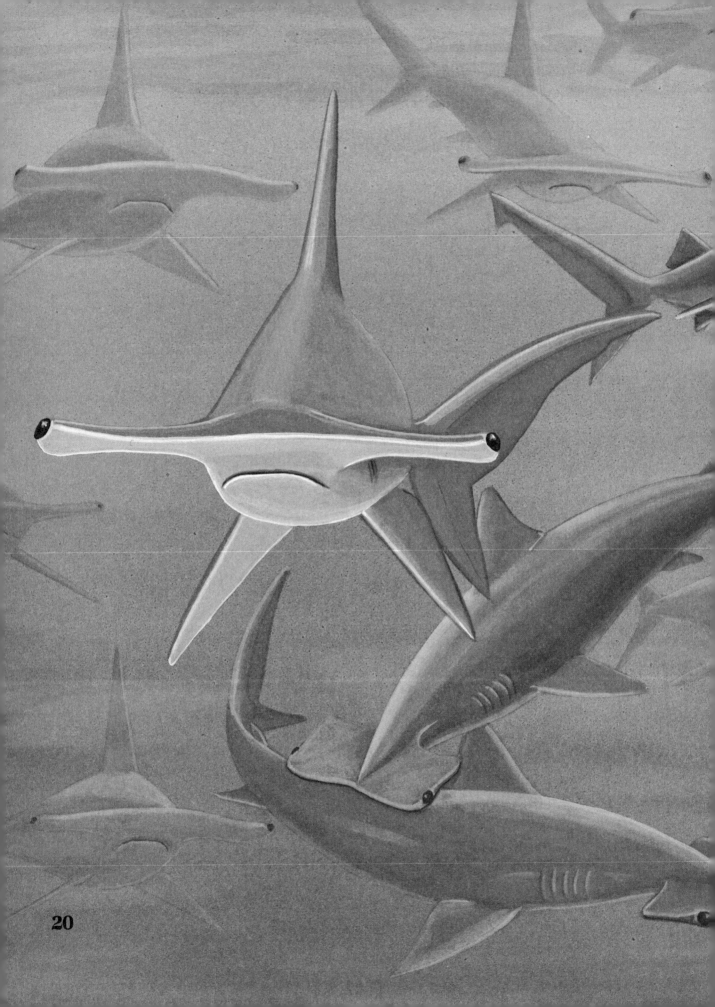

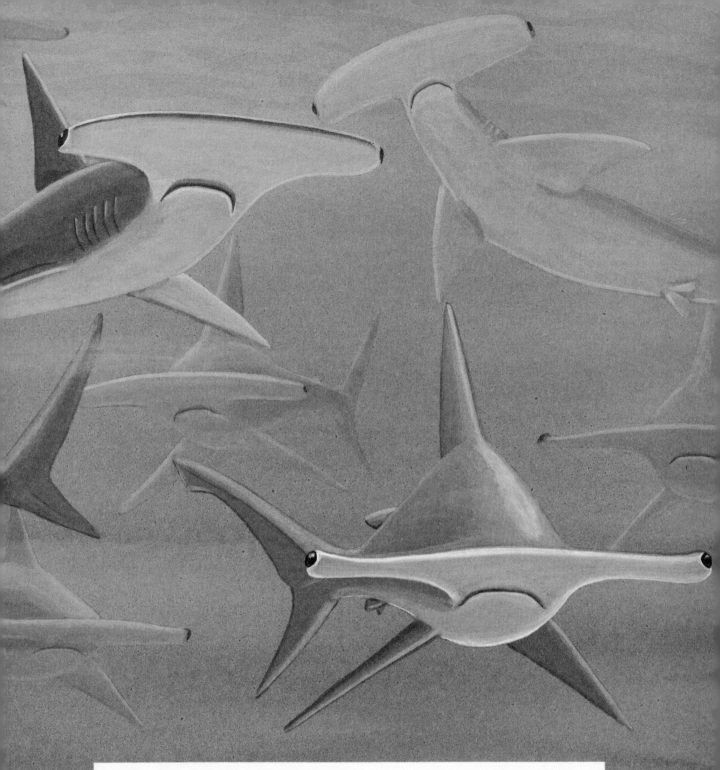

HAMMERHEAD SHARK Another big shark is the hammerhead shark. It can be 15 feet long and weigh 1000 pounds. Its eyes and its nostrils are at the end of its head. It can see backwards and forwards.

Hammerhead sharks swim in huge groups.

The tiger shark's egg case is also called a sea purse or mermaid's purse, or devil's pocketbook. Sometimes empty egg cases wash up on the beach.

OTHER SHARKS   Most sharks live in warm water. They eat almost anything, gulping it down whole. Once someone found three overcoats, a raincoat, and a car license plate in the stomach of a shark.

Most kinds of sharks are not dangerous to people. They eat fish and only attack people if people bother them.

Many people are afraid of sharks. They try to keep sharks away from beaches where there are swimmers. People have tried nets, explosions, air bubbles, suits of armor, and a chemical that smells like rotten shark to keep sharks away. Most of these things don't work well. But now scientists have discovered a fish that makes a chemical which most sharks seem to hate. Scientists are working on using this chemical to make a shark repellant.

People fish for sharks as a sport. In many countries people like to eat shark meat. The oil from the shark's liver is supposed to make people healthy. Shark skin with its sharp scales taken off is used to make shoes and handbags. Shark teeth are made into jewelry.

MAKO SHARK

LEMON
SHARK

LEOPARD SHARK

NURSE
SHARK

THRESHER SHARK

When there is blood in the water from a wounded sea creature, sharks seem to go crazy.
This is called a feeding frenzy. Many sharks gather and begin to bite and tear the body.
They get so wild they sometimes eat each other.

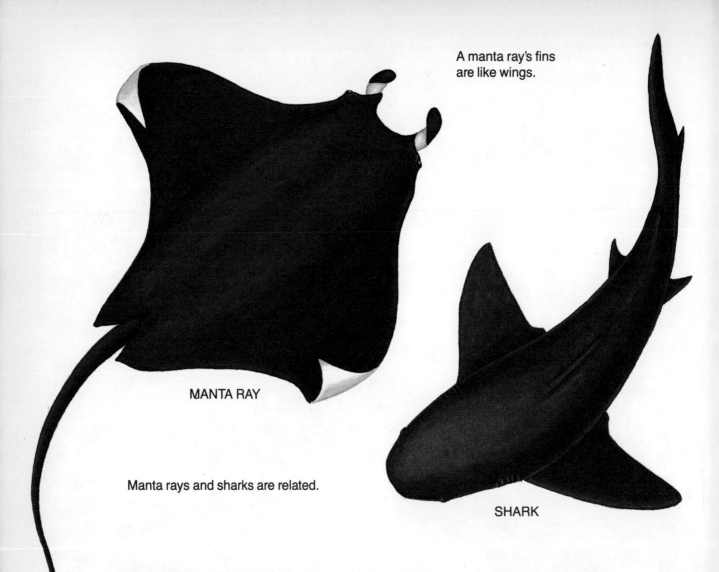

A manta ray's fins
are like wings.

MANTA RAY

Manta rays and sharks are related.

SHARK

MANTA RAY   The manta ray can grow as big as 22 feet from
the tip of one side fin to the tip of the other. It can weigh 3500
pounds. It is sometimes called the giant devilfish. It has two little
fins like horns on its head, and devils are supposed to have
horns. The fins are used to push floating food into the manta
ray's mouth.

The manta ray has a skeleton made of cartilage and rough
skin, just like a shark. It is like a flattened-out shark with bigger
side fins. Manta rays and sharks are related.

The manta ray is not dangerous to humans. It eats only small
sea animals. It opens its huge mouth. Then it swims through
crowds of little crabs, shrimps, and tiny sea animals, and eats
them.

Sometimes manta rays jump high out of the water.

Manta rays swim by flapping their large side fins. They look as if they are flying because the fins ripple up and down like wings. Manta rays often swim in groups. Sometimes many of them leap out of the water at the same time. They land in belly flops. The noise is like booms from a cannon.

One manta ray showed that it was not dangerous to people. It let a diver ride on its back.

Creatures of the Deep Seas

GIANT SPIDER CRAB   People do not often see the giant spider crab. People fishing sometimes catch it in their nets. It is the biggest crab of all. It has a leg span of ten feet and its body can measure one foot across. Not much else is known about it. It lives in very cold, deep waters off Japan.

Sometimes the male and female crabs shake hands for two or three weeks without stopping.

KING CRAB   A better-known large crab is the king crab. It lives in the sea off Alaska and Japan. It has a leg span of five feet and may weigh 20 pounds.

The king crab has ten legs. The back pair are small and folded out of sight. The front pair end in strong claws. The claws are so powerful that they can pinch halfway through a wooden broomstick.

Every so often king crabs get too big for their shells. A soft new shell grows inside the hard old one. Then the crab squeezes out of the old one. Getting rid of the old shell is called molting.

At mating time, the male king crab finds a female who is almost ready to molt. He holds her front legs with his claws. If the male wants to go somewhere, he takes the female with him. He holds her over his head as he hurries along.

King crabs are a very popular food all over the world. The meat that people eat is inside the legs and claws.

Baby king crabs are smaller than a pencil eraser. When they get to be about one and a half inches wide, thousands of young king crabs gather in bunches bigger than beach balls to protect themselves from enemies. When they are hungry they leave the bunch and go to feed. Then they all cling together again.

SWORDFISH

SWORDFISH   The swordfish is one of the biggest and fastest fish in the sea. It grows to be 15 feet long and can weigh 1200 pounds. It can swim 60 miles an hour, faster than many cars go on the highway. The swordfish hunts other fish for food. Herring, mackerel, and sardines are some of its favorite foods.

The sword of the swordfish is really its long upper jaw. Swordfish have no teeth and often use their sword to help them catch food. A swordfish swims into a group of smaller fish. It beats the fish with its sword until they are dead. Then it eats them.

The sword is also used to stab. Broken swords have been found in sharks, whales, and boats. Swordfish have attacked divers and submarines. If the sword breaks off, the swordfish doesn't grow a new one. A swordfish without a sword dies.

The swordfish beats smaller fish with its sword.

People like to fish for swordfish for sport because the swordfish are fierce fighters. Often they get away. Swordfish meat is eaten by people all over the world.

Baby swordfish hatch from eggs. The babies look different from their parents. They have two jaws of the same length and they have teeth. As they grow up, they grow a sword and lose their teeth.

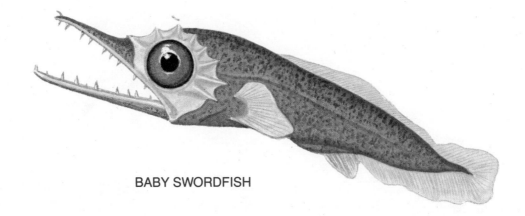

BABY SWORDFISH

SOME KINDS OF WHALES

BOWHEAD WHALE

CALIFORNIA GRAY WHALE

BLUE WHALE

30

Whales With Teeth

NARWHAL

SPERM WHALE

PORPOISE

ORCA

WHALES Whales are not fish. They are mammals. All whales must swim to the surface of the water to breathe air. There are 81 kinds of whales.

BOTTLENOSE DOLPHIN

31

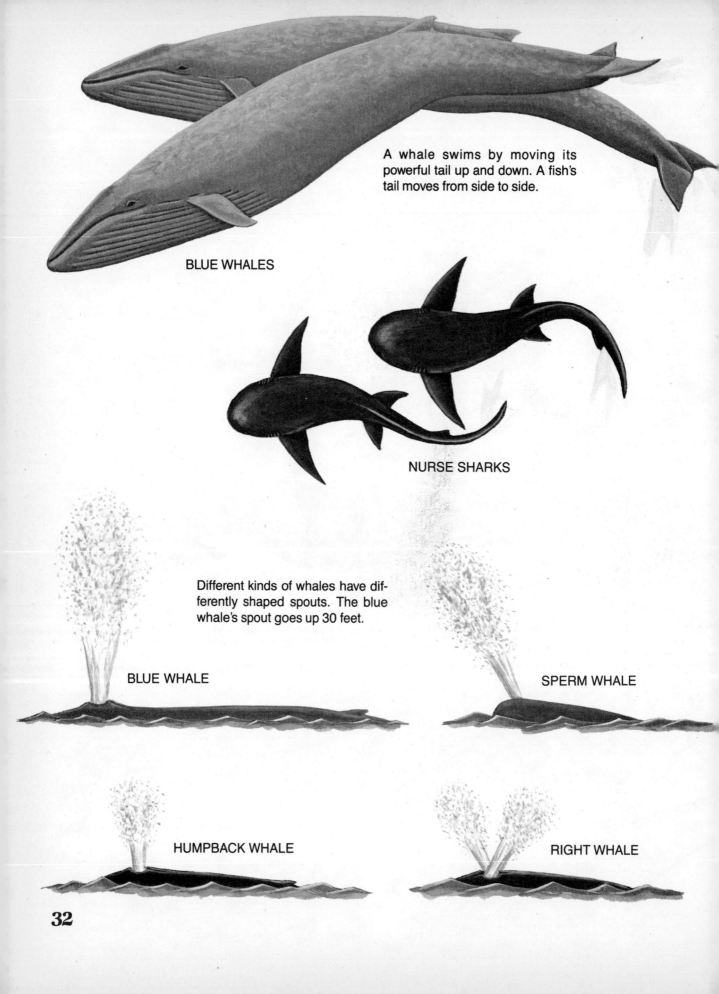

A whale swims by moving its powerful tail up and down. A fish's tail moves from side to side.

BLUE WHALES

NURSE SHARKS

Different kinds of whales have differently shaped spouts. The blue whale's spout goes up 30 feet.

BLUE WHALE

SPERM WHALE

HUMPBACK WHALE

RIGHT WHALE

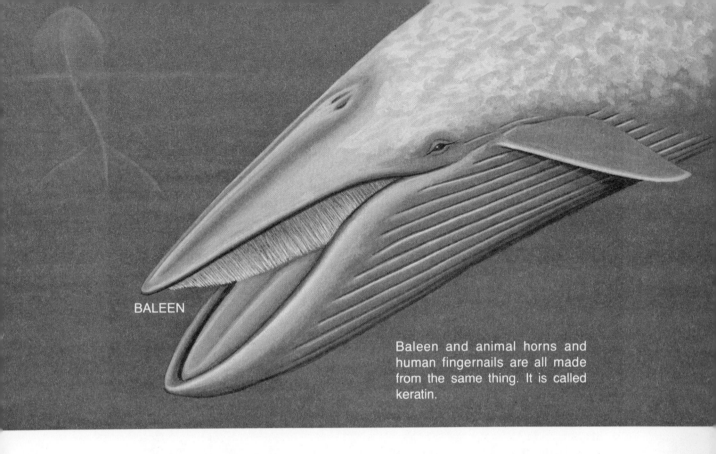

BALEEN

Baleen and animal horns and human fingernails are all made from the same thing. It is called keratin.

BLUE WHALE   The blue whale is the biggest animal that has ever lived. It can be 100 feet long and can weigh 120 tons. It is bigger than any dinosaur ever was. It weighs as much as 25 elephants. Its heart is as big as a small car.

The blue whale breathes through two nostrils just as people do. Its nostrils are on top of its head. They are called blowholes. Some kinds of whales have only one blowhole.

When the whale breathes out, the air coming out makes a mist. The mist is called the blow or spout.

Some whales have teeth. But the blue whale is a baleen whale. Baleen is a part of the blue whale's mouth. It is a material that hangs down from the blue whale's top jaw, instead of teeth. Baleen is like a strainer.

The blue whale swims along with its mouth open. It swims through crowds of sea animals called krill. The whale closes its mouth and presses up with its big tongue. Sea water is pushed out through the baleen strainer. The krill are left behind. In one meal a blue whale may eat two tons of krill.

BLUE WHALE BABIES   A blue whale calf is born in the water tail-first. Usually there is one baby. But sometimes twins are born.

The mother whale or another whale nearby helps the calf to the surface of the water. It breathes for the first time.

A blue whale calf weighs 4000 pounds at birth. It is 25 feet long. It drinks a ton of milk a day. In nine days it gains a ton. The calf doesn't have to suck to get the milk. It is squirted into the calf's mouth. The milk is very thick, like soft margarine.

The blue whale calf drinks its mother's milk for about eight months. Then it learns to find its own food in the ocean. The blue whale lives for about 50 years.

Blue whales and other baleen whales travel a long way every year. They start out from their feeding places. They swim to the places where they mate and calves are born. The California gray whale makes the longest trip of any mammal. It travels 12,000 miles every year.

The calf is helped
to the water's surface.

The blue whale calf is drinking milk.

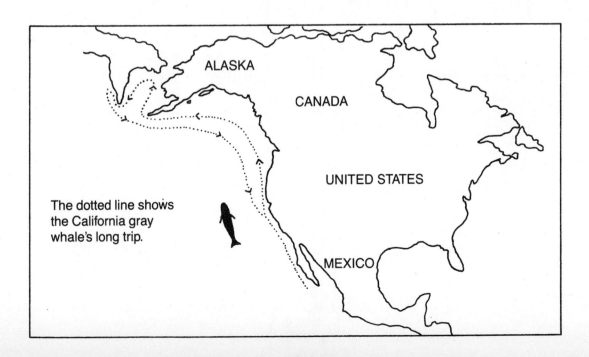

The dotted line shows the California gray whale's long trip.

ALASKA

CANADA

UNITED STATES

MEXICO

35

The humpback whale often jumps almost all the way out of the water.

HUMPBACK WHALE   The humpback whale is another baleen whale. It can be 50 feet long and weigh 45 tons. It has long flippers but no hump. It is named for the small fin on its back. On the humpback whale's head and jaw are dozens of bumps. Each bump has two bristly hairs sticking out of it.

Humpback whales eat krill. Sometimes the humpback whale traps krill in a very interesting way. The krill swim fast and are hard to catch. So the humpback whale blows a net of bubbles from its blowhole. The krill are captured in the middle of the bubbles and the whale eats them. Sometimes two whales together make a bubble net that is 100 feet across.

Humpback whales make noises that sound like singing. The songs are giant squeals and squeaks, huge bubbling groans, and deep slow roars. A song can last for half an hour. It can be heard by other whales for 100 miles underwater. Scientists think the songs are mating songs.

The humpback whale
makes a net of bubbles.

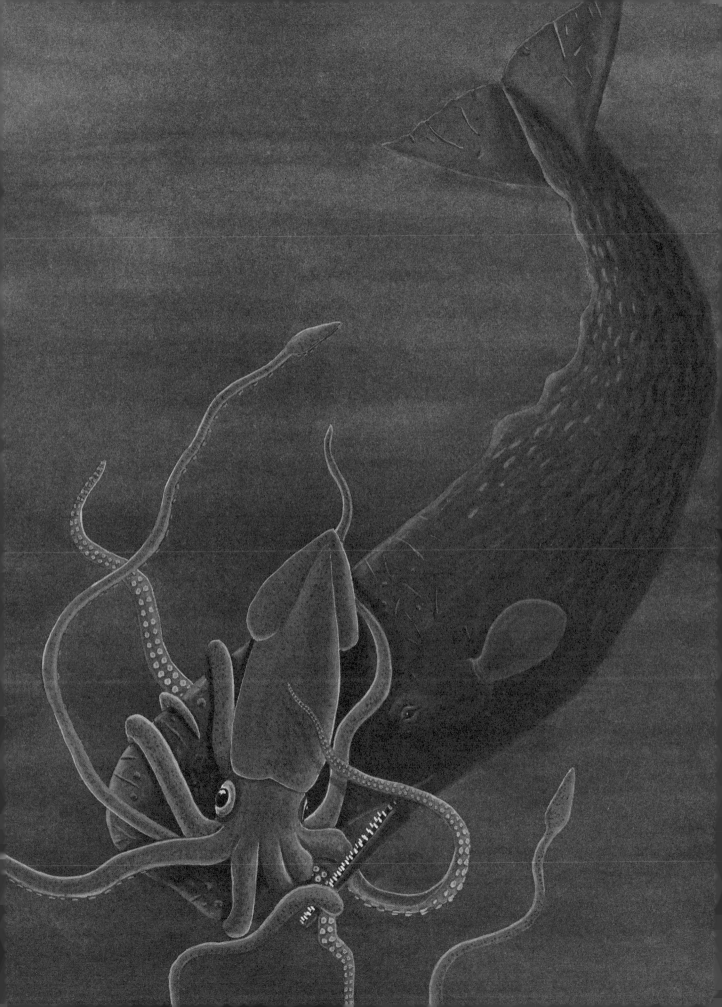

SPERM WHALE   The sperm whale is not a baleen whale. It is the biggest whale with teeth. It can be 60 feet long and can weigh 55 tons. It has 18 to 25 teeth on its lower jaw. The teeth are not sharp. They fit into holes in the upper jaw.

The sperm whale has a very big head. Almost one-third of its body is its head. It has one blowhole. It lives in the deep ocean where it can find its favorite food, the giant squid. It can stay underwater for as long as 90 minutes while it hunts and eats the squid.

Once a cable broke a mile under the ocean near South America. The cable carried telephone lines for overseas calls. The broken cable was pulled up. A dead whale was tangled in it. People guessed that the whale thought the cable was part of a giant squid.

Sperm whales often have round scars from the suckers on the arms of the giant squid. The scars are as big around as teacups.

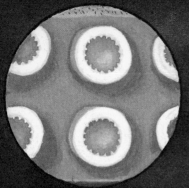

Each sucker on the giant squid's ten arms has a ring of horny teeth around it.

Creatures of the Very Deep Seas

GIANT SQUID The giant squid is related to the clam. It has a soft body with no bones. It has a small shell inside its body. It can grow to be 65 feet long and can weigh two tons.

The giant squid has the biggest eyes of any animal in the world. They are as big as Frisbees.

The giant squid has a beak like a parrot's. It tears at food with its beak. The squid has a tongue and teeth. It eats shrimp and fish such as mackerel and herring.

The giant squid moves by pulling water inside its body and then forcing it out through a tube beneath its head. The giant squid can squirt out a dark liquid like ink. The ink helps it escape from an enemy. The enemy sees the ink and thinks it is the squid. But the squid has gone away.

There are also little kinds of squids. Some people like to eat cut-up squid. Squids are also used as bait for fishing.

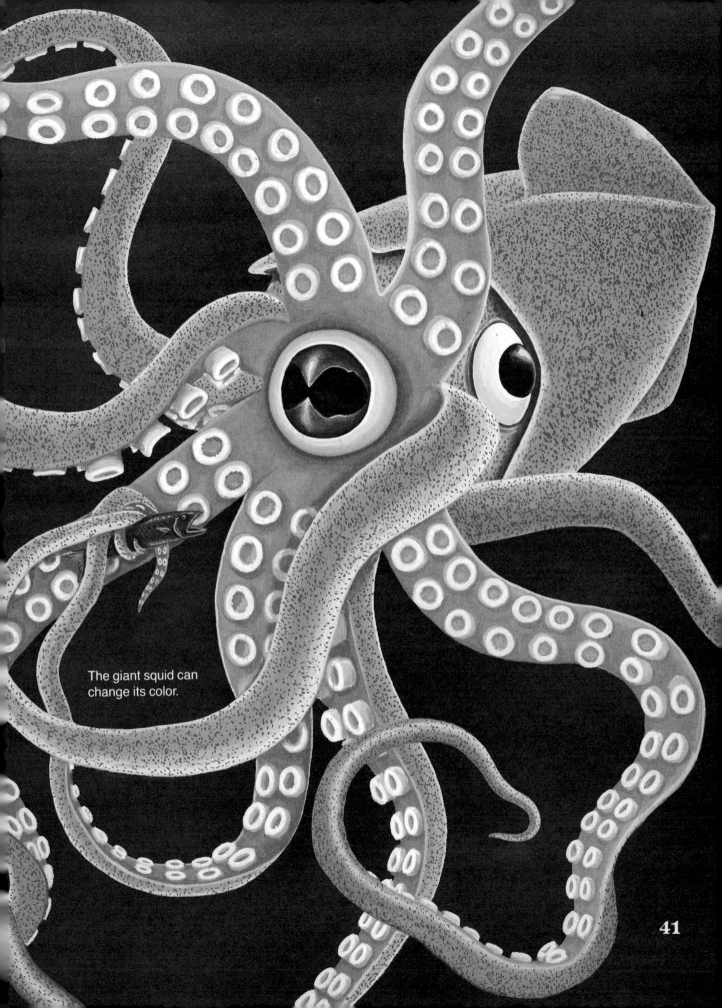

The giant squid can change its color.

Creatures of the Deepest Places

OARFISH   The oarfish lives about a mile below the water surface. It sometimes swims up to the top. The oarfish may be 20 feet long. Its body is very thin.

Below where the oarfish lives, the ocean is very cold and very dark. Animals that live in the deepest places are smaller than animals in shallower water.

Below two miles deep to seven miles deep at the bottom of the ocean there are no giant sea creatures. Only strange small fish live there. Most of them have body parts that shine in the blackness.

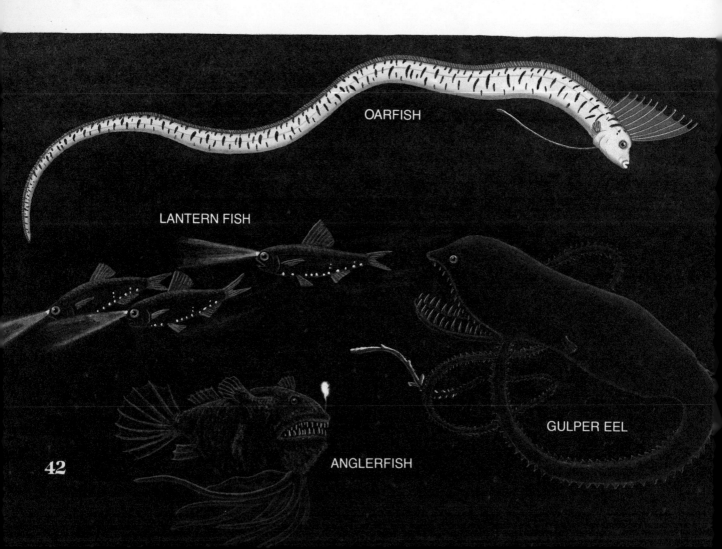

OARFISH

LANTERN FISH

GULPER EEL

ANGLERFISH

Scientists in the submarine
Alvin visited hot springs.

In a few places at the bottom of the sea there are jets of hot water. The hot water helps animals to grow big. Fat red worms that live in tubes, sea spiders one foot wide, and foot-long clams are some of the animals scientists have found.

Many of the giant creatures of the ocean are never seen by people, even if the people are sailors. But models of some can be seen in museums. Animals related to the giants may be seen in aquariums. Now more and more people are taking trips on the ocean to see whales. People who swim with a face mask or dive with tanks of air see large sea animals. And new giant creatures are still being discovered as humans keep on exploring under the sea.

Other Books About Sea Creatures

Books to read now

McGovern, Ann. *Little Whale*. New York: Scholastic Book Services, 1979.

Watson, Jane Werner. *Whales*. New York: Golden Press, 1975.

More difficult books to read later

Engel, Leonard. *The Sea*. Life Nature Library. New York: Time Incorporated, 1961, 1972.

Ommanney, F.D. *The Fishes*. Life Nature Library. New York: Time Incorporated, 1963.

About the Author and Artist

Edith Kunhardt has been writing ever since she can remember. Today, Ms. Kunhardt is the writer and editor of many popular books for children. Her article "Among the Whales in Mexico" was syndicated to 45 newspapers throughout the United States. Ms. Kunhardt has two grown children and lives in New York City.

Fiona Reid, born in England, studied science in college and graduate school. Ms. Reid feels that her training in science helps her to draw animals so they look real. She has never been to art school but has illustrated several books and other publications. Ms. Reid lives in Setauket, New York.

Index

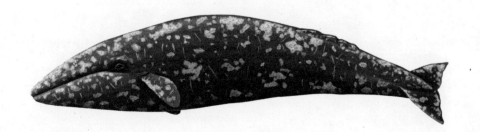